ARCHITECTURE & DESIGN LIBRARY

ENGLISH COUNTRY

ARCHITECTURE & DESIGN LIBRARY

ENGLISH COUNTRY

Julie Fowler

FRIEDMAN/FAIRFAX

PUBLISHERS

A FRIEDMAN/FAIRFAX BOOK

Library of Congress Cataloging-in-Publication Data

Fowler, Julie.
    English country   /   Julie Fowler.
                   p.   cm. --   (Architecture & design library ; 6)
    Includes index
    ISBN   1-56799-378-8
    1. Decoration and ornament, Rustic--England.   2. Country homes--England. 3. Interior decoration--England. I. Title   II. Series: Architecture and design library ; 6.
    NK2043.F683   1997
    747.22--dc20
                                            96-34594

Editor: Francine Hornberger
Art Director: Lynne Yeamans
Layout Design: Meredith Miller
Photography Editors: Samantha Larrance and Deidra Gorgos
Production Manager: Camille Lee

Color separations by Colourscan Overseas Co Pte Ltd
Printed and bound in the United States

1   3   5   7   9   10   8   6   4   2

For bulk purchases and special sales, please contact:
Friedman/Fairfax Publishers
Attention: Sales Department
15 West 26th Street
New York, New York 10010
212/685-6610 FAX 212/685-1307

Visit our website:
http://www.metrobooks.com

To my loving family, the Glossbrenners,
and all those who contributed to this book.

Contents

INTRODUCTION

Of all the great things that the English have invented and made part of the credit of the national character, the most perfect, the most characteristic, the only one they have mastered completely in all its details so that it becomes a compendious illustration of their social genius and their manners, is the well appointed, well administered, well filled country house.

—Henry James

If you are like me, Beatrix Potter's tales of Peter Rabbit or Frances Hodgson Burnett's *The Secret Garden* gave you your first impression of an English country house. Illustrations of both Mr. McGregor's humble farmhouse and vegetable garden, and Mary and Colin's Misselthwaite Manor with butlers, nannies, and a mysterious walled-in garden gave me an early feeling for the relationship between an English country house and its surroundings. Whether great in size and provenance, with an exquisitely designed garden of climbing roses and clipped boxwoods, or simple in stature and plainly picturesque, the relationship between the English country house and garden represents an essential aspect of English country life.

While the English country house and garden are the center of English country life, the family is the true heart of English country style. In the film adaptation of Jane Austen's *Sense and Sensibility*, the luxurious atmosphere of the Dashwoods' mansion evokes the idea of family because the rooms were created by the family's ancestral heritage. Generations of the privileged Dashwood family lived in the same house, creating layer upon layer of years of collections. A combination of architectural styles, decorating styles, furniture, and objects filled the rooms and gave the family a connection to their heritage. When Mrs. Dashwood and her daughters had to leave their estate and move into a smaller home, they were leaving more than just their house. By moving they were actually leaving a part of their family behind.

English country houses usually reveal their great age and have less than perfect interiors. Even in the wealthiest household, upholstery might be faded, painted surfaces dulled by the patina of age, and spaces crammed with old furniture and objects. There is a casual commingling of periods, styles, patterns, and colors. Well-chosen furniture, fabrics, and accessories show an appreciation for the antique. A

OPPOSITE: *A thatched-roof cottage in the Cotswolds defines the English ideal of a country retreat because of the way it is integrated into its rural surroundings. Climbing ivy adds to the overall effect.*

combination of shabbiness and luxury is the true nature of English country style decorating.

Masculine-looking book-lined walls make up libraries, and drawing rooms with a feminine feel are arranged with fine period furniture and decorated with gold-framed oil portrait paintings and yards of chintz fabrics. Ornamented fireplace mantels are presided over by classical busts and Chinese porcelains, and windows give views onto improbably vast and luxurious expanses of green lawns—all ideals of English country style.

TO THE MANOR BORN:
THE HISTORY OF THE ENGLISH COUNTRY HOUSE

In the Middle Ages, the English country house was built as a testament to a family's power and prestige. Passed down through the first-born male line, the country house symbolized the continuity of established families who resided in the same house for generations. It was typically filled with portraits of family, powerful friends, monarchs, and classical heroes.

In the centuries following the Renaissance, an essential part of a young gentleman's education was to take an extensive sight-seeing European Grand Tour, during which he would collect large amounts of objects and furniture. These would serve as reminders of his trip when he returned to England. Classical busts, oil paintings of great classical scenes, marble inlay tables, tapestries, carpets, furniture, blue and

RIGHT: *An English country living room is both elegant and cozy, stylized and eclectic. Turquoise-colored walls enliven the room's somber beige patterned upholstery and carpeting. An identical pair of sofas strewn with throw pillows sits fireside. A built-in book shelf has an unusual Art Deco–style pediment and enshrines groupings of china plates, vases, bowls, and figurines. Framed pictures defy the laws of gravity, hanging flat against the slanted wall.*

white porcelains, and even architectural drawings to use to create his country manor were the souvenirs of his jaunts. In combination with new, well-chosen pieces of quality and style, these souvenirs comprise the collections found in great English country houses today.

The vast economic and social changes wrought by the Industrial Revolution led to urbanization and the growth of a prosperous middle class. By the mid-nineteenth century, the country house was a refuge from fast-paced London life. The country house offered an escape from the city and an opportunity to cultivate leisure time. Hunting and fishing, drawing and painting, and musical pursuits, literature, games, and eating, as well as afternoon tea with biscuits and jam, fox hunts, and polo matches typify the activities enjoyed at the country house.

The grand style of the wealthiest English country households was determined by the current fashion of the period. The latest architectural developments, imported fabrics, and furniture were sought with a fervor. The lifestyles of the wealthiest were eagerly adopted by the merely affluent, and it is these humbler versions of the grand country manors that truly reflect the grace and charm that is the hallmark of the great English country house.

Today, the National Trust owns and preserves many of England's oldest, most impressive country houses. Often these properties are museumlike—completely preserved encapsulations of the era of manservants, housemaids, and footmen. Their legacy, however, the time-honored style known as "English Country"—is much more liveable. In the pages that follow, you will find numerous examples of this comfortable, eclectic, lived-in style that so perfectly combines past and present—and may inspire you to create your own version of English Country.

ABOVE: *A functional stainless steel sink sits atop recycled barn siding for a true farmhouse effect. The chipped paint and crumble-down look is enhanced by fresh-cut wildflowers in an old clay pitcher. Potted geraniums catch sunlight from a window with a garden view that brightens the task of dishwashing.*

A B O V E : *A vaulted glass ceiling provides a generous amount of sunlight for the healthy growth of flowering vines. The bright, patterned fabric on a round central table and easy chairs echoes the floral theme of the room and adds a splash of color. Extra seating is provided in the form of mismatched wooden chairs casually placed around the table.*

CHAPTER ONE

HOUSE AND GARDEN

The English country house comes in many variations of style and size. Regal greystone manors sit majestically atop green meadows. Large classical structures with a regular pattern of windows and a large portico reflect Italian palazzos, while towering masses of half-timbered walls, thatched roofs, and diamond-mullioned windows are indicative of classic cottage style. Organic building materials such as brick, stone, stucco, and wood together with thatched roofs and decorative wisps of climbing ivy combine to make these houses look as if they were carved out of the lush English countryside.

England's verdant countryside has spawned generations of passionate gardeners, and cultivation of the exteriors of country houses has become an art form. Embellishments of climbing vines and flowers further integrate country houses into the landscape. The classic image of a country cottage with roses adorning the front door can be found on both the grandest manor house and the humblest thatched cottage. This combination of natural building materials and natural adornments establishes for the architecture a feeling of oneness with nature.

Avid travelers, the English have brought home many great ideas from other cultures and adapted them to their own. Inspirations from France and Italy led to England's grand-style symmetrical gardens. Grottos, picturesque vistas, fake ruins, pergolas, and manmade ponds set around circuitous paths set the standard for English garden design. Ideas were also imported to the country from the city and further adapted to fit the lifestyle of the country—the idea of melding architecture and nature together started not in the country but in London.

Indoor/outdoor spaces such as patios and porches are essential to English country living as they provide the opportunity to enjoy gardens and the countryside within a semi-enclosed, private space. Lounging the afternoon away on a wisteria-covered patio on a lazy summer day, or dining in a glass conservatory that stretches out into magnificent gardens are just a couple of the many true pleasures of English country living.

OPPOSITE: *A Georgian-style brick manor house majestically presides over idyllic estate grounds. The house's reflection on the water complements both architecture and nature.*

RIGHT: *An inviting two-story classic cottage has a thatched roof with opposing chimneys whose fireplaces are used to warm both sides of the cozy house. A central front door is embellished with an arched trellis that helps support the generous climbing vines that decorate the façade.*

ABOVE: *The front of a country house of classic Palladian proportions is completely covered with creeping vines. The freshly painted white windows and front door show that the vines are the deliberately unclipped embellishments of an otherwise well-maintained manor.*

ABOVE: *An English garden bursts with a complementary mix of flora in bright colors. Backed by a privet hedge, the combination of pink, raspberry, violet, yellow, and orange blossoms creates a joyful display.*

RIGHT: *A privet hedge is pierced by a picket gate and an arched trellis with red climbing roses. The low-hung gate allows a view into the enclosed, enchanting garden.*

ABOVE: *The owner's green thumb has made a simple stone cottage romantic and inviting. A lush front border garden is presided over by the bright red flowers of climbing vines and hanging container plants. The cottage's many windows give its inhabitants a connection to the outside.*

BELOW: *The hard edges of a tall, mullioned window are softened by outlines of English wisteria. A family's heraldry appears in the geometric design of the windowpanes to identify the houses's original residents.*

ABOVE: *A teak bench with a curvilinear design is situated for its unobstructed view of a terraced backyard. A wicker basket used to carry the accoutrements of a busy gardener is filled with fresh-cut flowers and a wide-brimmed hat.*

LEFT: *A hexagonal brick folly was originally built as a hunting lodge or getaway cottage on the grounds of a large manor. Hipped-roof projections add space to the interior. Blue-painted windows and door add visual interest and create a contrast between the red bricks and green grass.*

RIGHT: *Matisse painted trees like these, their slender beauty providing a supremely elegant backdrop for a simple arrangement of French iron garden chairs around a square outdoor table. The harmony between the brick terraces and manicured hedges can be appreciated from the garden furnishings used as a stop-off during strolling or working in this pastoral setting.*

RIGHT: *A charming pavilion, newly erected for secluded outdoor entertaining, provides visitors with a covered venue for contemplation of a manicured backyard. A terrace is created by a sloping stone wall behind a low-growing bed of foliage. New trees were planted for future generations to enjoy.*

A B O V E : *A manor house's façade was designed with a balanced arrangement of windows set neatly within unembellished stone walls. Informal-style landscaping surrounds the house and connects it to the surrounding countryside.*

A B O V E : *A conservatory pulsating with life is filled with plants, flowers, and Victorian-style wicker and iron furniture. Natural woven shades block the strong sun of high noon and can be rolled up as the day goes on. A terra-cotta floor allows for easy cleanup of water spills and of the grass and dirt that are inevitably dragged in from the outside.*

ABOVE: *A simple stone cottage has an interesting Moorish-style pediment on stylized columns. The plain landscaping and the pureness of the façade have the appeal of modern-day minimalism.*

RIGHT: *A typical English country cottage, the strongly graphic feel of this house and outbuilding contrasts with its informally landscaped setting. A front yard moat is crossed by a covered bridge with a second story to match the height of the main house.*

CHAPTER TWO
ROOMS FOR COMFORTABLE LIVING

English country style interiors may not always appear to be organized, but underlying the seemingly undisciplined mix of periods, patterns, and colors are principles of balance and harmony. The result is an overall attractive and comfortable impression. You may find such natural elements as flagstone floors; woven natural floor matting; half-timbered and brick walls; and fabrics of cotton, wool and silk. Colors of the earth, from russet reds to deep leafy greens, the pale yellows of flowers, and light sky blues brighten English country style rooms. Patterns inspired by nature show up on fabric, porcelain, carpets, and wall stencils, bringing the garden indoors. Walls may feature hunting prints, landscape paintings, or Victorian etchings, all layered atop a floral wallpaper.

The charm and timelessness of English country style endure because the best rooms of this style all pay great attention to detail. From the tiniest tassel to the plumpest sofa, from fresh-cut flowers to a fruit still-life in a blue and white porcelain bowl, the details of English country style are paramount. John Fowler of Colefax & Fowler, the most influential decorator of the English country house look, was known for his unmatched attention to decorative and architectural detail. He developed an exquisite balance of color, pattern, and fantasy in his English country style rooms, which is probably why these rooms are as celebrated today as when they were first created.

The attention to detail begins in the front hall, the introduction to a house. Its importance dates from the Middle Ages when it served wealthy families as reception room, living room, and dining hall. A family's heraldry and armor were displayed as embellishment and as an announcement of identity. Tapestries were hung to display wealth and to insulate the hall from drafts. Later, the development of wooden wainscoting for insulation provided a backdrop for the minimal furnishings of boards on trestles and benches, which were used for easy setup and removal from the multifunctional space.

In later years, the great hall remained the center of the English country house, but the need for privacy led to the addition of private second-floor quarters with drawing rooms for intimate meetings. Over centuries, the layout of the house changed from a large central hall into a collection of rooms on separate floors. From this arrangement developed the classic country house layout of a living room and dining

OPPOSITE: *A multilayered decorating scheme reflects additions made over time in this living room. A mixing of unrelated patterns and styles and a jumble of various accessories throughout defines this room's eclectic style. Draped plaid fabric over the table top and sofa has a homespun appeal.*

room flanking a central hall with bedrooms and bathrooms upstairs. Over time, separate hallways, libraries, galleries, and drawing rooms were added for the comfort of country house inhabitants.

In today's country house, the front hallway retains its importance for setting a welcoming tone for guests. It is usually furnished with restraint and a sense of formality, with attention to its practical function. The English weather is tracked in through both front and back doors, and a place to sit and remove boots, a stand in which to stow umbrellas, and a rack on which to hang coats are important features. Hardwood, flagstone, brick, tiled, or slate floors are common. Walls may be white or painted plaster, half-paneled, wallpapered, and hung with pictures. Furniture is usually kept to a minimum. A console table with matching chairs may be surmounted by a large mirror, and provides a good surface on which to toss mail and keys.

The English country living room provides a refuge for leisurely pursuits and common functions of the house. In smaller houses, the living room may also include a small dining area, and be lined with bookshelves if a separate library does not exist. An overall timeless feeling of comfort and relaxation is created by a casual mixing of complementary fabric patterns and colors, set within the unifying influence of a harmonious color scheme. Old furniture predominates and mixes with well-chosen new pieces. Sun-faded window treatments and tattered upholstery add lived-in charm. The focus of the living room is often the central fireplace. Furniture and objects balanced around the fireplace add grace and harmonize disparate pieces into the scheme.

The final design touch in the English country room is often a collection of cherished objects. Continually added-to collections and objects with meaning, inherited or newly acquired, create tabletop displays, make a statement about an owner's style, and will probably become treasured heirlooms.

ABOVE: *A neatly furnished hallway leads outdoors to a flagstone terrace and the garden beyond. Walking sticks fill an umbrella stand next to a unique wooden side chair. A classic English equestrian oil painting hangs above the wainscoting on available wall space. An heirloom grandfather clock's case reveals the fine grain of its highly polished veneer.*

ABOVE: *An exposed beam ceiling with whitewashed walls pierced by diamond-mullioned leaded windows makes a quaint backdrop for an informal living room. The antique style of the new sofa is lent authenticity by time-worn and faded upholstery. Muted color, decorative fringe, and cording enrich the comfortable furnishings.*

ABOVE: *A quietly elegant entryway is tastefully decorated with a neat*
display of stylish brimmed hats and an arrangement of walking sticks and
umbrellas in an oversized urn. Hanging binoculars anticipate the next
birdwatching trip. Coats and boots are kept behind a closet door fitted with
medieval-style hardware.

BELOW: *A Gothic castle becomes a work of art in itself when framed by this deep-set, arched doorway in this English country home. An antique birdcage is a delicate touch.*

ABOVE: *An absence of strong patterns or colors in this room emphasizes objects and furnishings and helps to create a fresh living environment. In the spirit of English country decorating, three blue-and-white platters draw attention to the room's high ceiling. Other collected pieces decorate a table on which keys and mail may be tossed.*

ABOVE: *A painted cabinet houses a country collection of table linens and is conveniently positioned for outdoor dining and picnic use. The color of the cabinet is echoed by a harmony of complementary objects and artwork hung on the white plaster and exposed stone wall.*

LEFT: *The purposefully casual arrangement of slipcovered furniture creates an undecorated feeling for comfort in this spacious living room. Peripheral areas are filled with bookshelves, tables, and writing desks which show the many functions of the accommodating space. An ancestral portrait presides majestically over the fireplace.*

OPPOSITE: *Natural woven seagrass matting, celadon wainscoting, and built-ins create a fresh looking library. A large slipcovered ottoman in beige and cream is used as a coffee table and for storage of more reading material. The "less is more" decorating approach brings a relaxed airiness to the well-filled space, and keeps the books the focus of the room.*

TOP, RIGHT: *Sometimes an English country house is not large enough to accommodate a separate library. Here, a makeshift library was created in a small outbuilding when a leather bookshelf border was nailed on the edge of a farmhouse table and shelves overstuffed with books were added.*

BOTTOM, RIGHT: *Virtually all available space is filled in this combination hallway and library. A sofa crosses the doorway, thus connecting two rooms and making them one. Spillover shelves store a vast collection of books.*

LEFT: *The real accoutrements of an active English country life inhabit the back entrance area of this home. An ever-evolving utilitarian space hosts rubber wellies, firewood, garden clippers, and a hand-basket for weekend chores, along with the large house's impressive set of keys.*

OPPOSITE: *Garden style gives an entryway its decorating theme. Framed botanical prints and terra-cotta pots filled with flowers and topiaries grace the space. A vine border, floral-patterned curtain treatment, and woven seagrass floor matting complete the verdant motif.*

OPPOSITE: *A balanced display of skirted tables with matching accessories and hanging pictures flanks a Tudor-style fireplace with a carved overhead decoration that organizes the great room. An oversized ottoman upholstered in tapestry and a sofa with a matching pair of throw pillows sit on an Aubusson carpet that enriches the space with its coloration and formidable size.*

TOP, RIGHT: *Furniture and personal objects, including a rolltop desk, dried flowers, and antique prints, enrich this space. A plain beige wall-to-wall carpet is enhanced by a worn needlepoint rug of great character and charm.*

BOTTOM, RIGHT: *Outfitted for the realistic features of English country life, the flagstone floor of an entryway hall provides for the trudging in of rain- or mud-soaked boots. Umbrellas are conveniently stowed doorside. Candle lanterns provide illumination when the door is closed and at night, as well as antique charm.*

RIGHT: *A cool white living room is decked out in a blue and white color scheme. A shabby-chic sofa is covered with a faded checkerboard quilt and strewn with square throw pillows of coordinating patterns. Gold accents warm the room and imbue it with a sense of glamour. It is this combination of comfort and elegance that defines the English country ideal.*

BELOW: *In this cozy living room, well-coordinated mismatched fabrics cover worn-out furnishings and flea market finds serve to imbue the decor with charm.*

OPPOSITE: *A plush Chesterfield creates an inviting backdrop for three neatly placed throw pillows of uniform size. The high windowsill is a good stage for a balanced display of heirloom statuettes. A single vase of fresh flowers echoes the porcelain flower arrangement under a glass dome and breathes life into the decor.*

LEFT: *The paraphernalia of sport and daily life inhabit this warmly colored hallway. A passion for birds and butterflies is evident from the objects preserved under glass.*

ABOVE: *A larger sized country house still has housebells, once used to summon servants, left over from its grand past. To avoid confusion and ensure prompt attention, each room had its own bell.*

LEFT: *The walls of this staircase are papered in a two-tone beige-striped pattern and hung with a large series of simply framed bird prints that invoke a country feel. The wide-stripe pattern reinforces the verticality of the walls and double height of the ceiling.*

LEFT: *A balustraded stairway landing is a large enough space in which to position an antique carved table. In addition to its ornamental purpose, the table is a wonderful surface to display a flower arrangement held in a classic Arts and Crafts ceramic vase.*

ABOVE: *The center of an informal living room plays host to an oversized tufted settee with a rolled back. Upholstered in pale floral cotton chintz with a twisted silk cord, the settee adds romantic quirkiness to the rural interior.*

ABOVE: *A matching pair of table lamps and paintings on both sides of a window help to structure a large home office and sitting room, but the seemingly unorganized mix of furniture gives the feeling that the space is filled with the leftovers of a very large household.*

ABOVE: *A floor-to-ceiling window presides over a subtly dramatic room built to look like an old manor house. Exposed beams and stone pierce the plaster walls, creating a rustic ambience. Simple furnishings and accessories accent the "lodge" feel of the space.*

LEFT: *An invitingly comfortable living room is traditionally appointed with upholstered furniture in coordinating patterns and colors. Various floral patterns on the throw pillows and window treatments, and on the ottoman that serves as a coffee table, connect with each other to unify the room. The blue easy chair is a cool contrast to the warm-hued upholstery set against enveloping yellow walls.*

RIGHT: *A montage of black-and-white engravings and small oil paintings creates a focal point on a sunflower yellow sitting room wall. A mix of textile patterns having a predominantly red color scheme enriches the dark grain of the wood furniture and handsome desk clock.*

ABOVE: *An enormous second-story window reveals an estate's well-manicured grounds and the breathtaking mountainous coastline. The window itself is a work of art—no curtains or other embellisments are needed to enhance its beauty.*

CHAPTER THREE

KITCHENS AND DINING ROOMS

In the earliest English country houses, meals were ceremoniously presented to the family in the great hall, which also functioned as the dining room. Formal presentation rituals are still performed today, and the idea of ceremony still exists, even in middle class country houses: dinner guests and family members are expected to dress when dinner is served in the main dining room.

As times changed, dining in smaller parties became more desirable, as it was an honor to be selected to share a meal with a small party. Instead of dining in the great hall, the meal was served at a small gateleg table in a corner of the living room. Today's smaller country houses may not always have the luxury of a separate dining room. In modest houses, a scrubbed pine table in a corner of the kitchen will be used instead. In slightly larger houses, dining rooms adjacent to the kitchen that were built originally for servants are used. They may be furnished with ordinary pieces arranged in a practical, rather than fancy, manner.

Formal dining rooms used mostly for entertaining retain a place of importance in the house. A large oak table surrounded by a matching suite of chairs is the focal point of the room. A sideboard is used as a buffet surface, and a tall breakfront houses the family's china and table linens. A silver tea set and candlesticks decorate tabletops and add a touch of glamour to the room. Paintings, mirrors, matching pairs of wall sconces, and plates adorn walls. Often a beautiful crystal chandelier hangs over the table. An oriental rug, patterned carpet, or natural woven matting is an appropriate covering for a hardwood floor, while damask draperies may serve to accent windows.

In medieval country houses, kitchens were mostly separate from the formal dining area. Meals were cooked over open fires and the kitchen would often become too sooty and greasy in which to dine comfortably. To help ventilation, these rooms were built with high ceilings.

Today, the kitchen is the hub of the English country house. Besides being the place where a family's food is prepared, family and friends often relax here to share meals and sip tea. Regardless of size, English country kitchens always display a well-organized use of space often including natural pine or painted wood fitted cabinets for maximum storage. If more room is needed, there will often be a separate

OPPOSITE: *Trompe l'oeil sheaves of wheat painted around the mantel create a focal point in this dining room. The pale blue mantelpiece complements the color of checked cushions that soften the hardness of wooden chairs. Blue and white china set out for serving matches a small collection on a round side table.*

pantry or scullery to house washers and dryers, a freezer, and more shelving for storing food and tools. A scrubbed pine table is the focal point of many country kitchens and windows are usually hung with gingham or other homespun fabric curtains.

Built-in open shelving and plate racks display large collections of hanging cups, pitchers, plates, and platters. Baskets hanging from the ceiling next to dried herbs, a rectangular pine table with a bouquet of fresh-cut wildflowers, and a suite of painted wooden chairs with rush seats are classic embellishments. Matching window treatments and seat cushions help tie a kitchen's decorative scheme together and unify the environment of disparate tools and objects.

The Aga cooker is often the heart of the English country kitchen and is visually appropriate where modern appliances like refrigerators and dishwashers are best hidden behind cabinet doors. The Aga provides a variety of cooking facilities, as well as a place for drying wet laundry, and possibly heating most of the house's radiators. The Aga may be powered by gas, oil, or electricity, and comes in many different sizes and a broad range of bright enameled colors to coordinate with any scheme.

ABOVE: *The diamond pattern of exterior leaded windows as seen through more contemporary window panes creates a feeling of the past mixing with the present—typical of English country style. Scrubbed wood countertops coordinate with the interior window set in a pure white plaster wall. Only unfinished wood and natural-toned objects exist within the picturesque kitchen.*

OPPOSITE: *Butcher-block countertops are conveniently situated beneath a window providing a brightly lit workspace. A hint of a rectangular washbasin is seen opposite an Aga that matches the creamy color of the walls. Green tiles, a traditional surface material, cover the lower portion of the wall and introduce color to the room. Colorful pots are displayed as decorative elements as well as for practical accessibility.*

LEFT: *Eighteenth-century mahogany chairs, a dining table for eight, gold-framed oil portraits, and well-chosen decorative accessories comprise this dining room painted an unusual shade of deep teal. A red velvet upholstered easy chair with a standing floor lamp coordinates with the warm color of the curtains, but is a curious addition to an otherwise traditionally furnished room.*

ABOVE: *Ice blue combines with natural tones to create an eclectic, yet harmonious feel in this country kitchen.*

ABOVE: *A whimsical procession of mounted horses and hunting dogs parades above the architrave in a double-height dining room flooded with natural sunlight. Sky-blue walls echo the clear sky above. The red tablecloth provides a warm contrast to the coolness of the cobalt blue chairs and coordinates with the adjacent sun-bathed living room.*

ABOVE: *A neo-Gothic style conservatory makes a dramatic setting for a warm-weather dining room. Two sets of double doors lead outside to a private terrace surrounded by thick foliage where the fresh flowers that embellish the table were cut. The green and white plaid seat cushions on iron dining chairs and matching tablecloth echo the color scheme of the outdoors.*

OPPOSITE: *A display of mostly white objects in a well-designed, all-cream compact kitchen is strategic for maximizing the sense of space. Glass canisters neatly display flour, sugar, and other foodstuffs on organized shelves. A pristine white tea service is set up for the traditional English afternoon ritual.*

RIGHT: *In the corner of a rustic alley kitchen, shelves display utilitarian equipment and food. Airtight containers and apothecary jars provide see-through storage of food staples. Cutting boards, pots, pans, and rolling pins are set underneath the wood countertop for easy access.*

ABOVE: *A pristine country kitchen's creamy yellow cupboards and door create the backdrop for a sturdy table and antique wood chairs. A restrained use of accessories evokes a lived-in quality without seeming cluttered. Cookbooks, potted plants, and glasses are openly displayed, breaking up the regularity and modern look of wood-fronted cabinets.*

ABOVE: *An informal country kitchen is embellished with collections of the practical objects used there. A hanging display of linens, platters, and plates and a suite of covered pots coordinate with a prevailing blue-and-white color scheme. The table is spread with a white linen tablecloth and the chairs are relaxed with soft blue-and-white-check seat cushions. An old hearth is a nook for a glass-fronted storage cabinet that holds cookbooks and the family's china.*

ABOVE: *Balloon-back dining chairs, heirloom-style table linens, and antique furniture set within the muted colors of an adjoining living room and dining room create an old-world atmosphere. A traditionally set dining table befits the graceful interior.*

OPPOSITE: *The great age of this country house reveals the progressive use of a hallway over time. Designed and decorated as a formal passageway, this hall has a Palladian window and arched pediment. Gold-framed portraits hung gallery-style on paneled walls make for an impressive entrance to the dining room. Both the masonry floor in slight disrepair and the faded upholstery of the chairs express a casual attitude. Everyday objects adorning a small table further evidence that the hall is no longer exclusively used as walk-through space.*

BELOW: *The close proximity of a dining area to the adjacent kitchen suggests that it is privately used by the homeowners rather than reserved for formal entertaining. A casual mixing of greens on the walls, moldings, chairs, and tablecloth unifies the room in a relaxed style. An eclectic mix of objects—terracotta pots, candlesticks and a teapot on the mantel, a hanging empty birdcage, and paintings resting on the molding—shows a casual country decorating approach.*

ABOVE: *Creative use of available space sets this four-oven Aga neatly under the rounded Tudor arch of an original hearth. A pair of bracketed side-shelves for tea and spices are small-scale versions of the mantel shelf that provides open storage for a cook's collection of pots. Baskets used to carry in fresh vegetables and herbs from the garden are suspended "out of the way." A painting overhead shows that there is never an inappropriate place to display art.*

ABOVE: *The rustic atmosphere of a ground-floor dining room suggests the style of an old English pub. A fireplace flanked by a matching pair of candle sconces, and a candle chandelier overhead show the owner's preference for firelight over electric. The plaster between the exposed beams of the ceiling is painted a deep red to complement the green color of the door, grandfather clock, and ceramic wall tiles.*

CHAPTER FOUR

BEDROOMS, NURSERIES, AND BATHROOMS

Until the late Middle Ages, bedrooms tended to be a perquisite of the wealthy, and no piece of furniture was more coveted or more expensive than the bed. These beds were often massive wooden structures, ornately carved, and perhaps even bearing the family coat-of-arms. To provide privacy from servants who may have been sharing the bedchamber, and in colder climates to ensure warmth, the bed was often heavily draped with ornate tapestries or imported velvet, damask, or silk. In later eras, bed styles evolved to incorporate canopies, paneled or upholstered head- and footboards, posts, and other decorative elements. Today's English country bedrooms retain a sense of the past, with a fondness for canopies, draperies, and other bed hangings.

More than any other area of the house, the bedroom is designed to be a private space. In the bedroom, one is surrounded by cherished items that express one's most personal passions. The bedroom is a refuge from the busy world, a place to relax and shed the cares of the day.

English country style itself is all about comfort, so it is only natural that the English country bedroom is epitomized by words like casual, charming, and cozy. A wrought-iron, brass, or carved wooden bed, replete with canopy or four-postered and draped, provides the centerpiece around which the rest of the room's furnishings gather. Great attention is given to incorporating collections of fine bed linens,

layered for comfort and style, and topped with numerous plump pillows and cushions. Patchwork quilts, which may be family heirlooms, add unsurpassed country flavor. The mainstay of the English country look, mixed patterns and prints, manifests itself here in softly colored florals and stripes chosen for their gentle charm. Harmony is achieved in a unified decorative scheme of matching or complementary valances, curtains, wallpaper, and upholstered pieces.

Furniture in the bedroom is likely to include an armoire, as closets are rarely found in old houses, unless they were added at a later date; a chest of drawers, a trunk, and perhaps a small desk. Older wooden furniture that has fallen on hard times may get a new life from a coat of paint, stenciling, or a decorative paint treatment.

Accessorizing personal spaces is essential to creating an atmosphere of pure relaxation. Here, collections that are particularly

OPPOSITE: *Dual-purpose curtain panels on brass rods separate the bedroom from the bath and theatrically frame the large painting centered on the back wall. The generously sized white bed coverlet is echoed by the fabric draped over the bedside table round. Clutter has been kept to a minimum.*

precious may find the perfect site—cut crystal cosmetics jars with silver lids, perfume bottles, tortoiseshell hairbrushes and combs, antique shaving brushes—any of these might adorn a bedside table. Books, ubiquitous in an English country home, may be scattered casually or more formally arranged in scaled-down bookcases.

It was during the Victorian era that special care began to be taken in the decoration of nurseries and childrens rooms. Indeed, child-sized furniture and accessories are favorite collectibles among admirers of Victorian style. Today, an English country room for a baby might contain an old painted iron crib or pram, a white-painted wicker rocking chair, antique dolls or a dollhouse, and nineteenth-century prints. For a childs room, collections of toys and books, a painted wooden floor, and scattered throw rugs evoke the mixed-up comfort of English country without too much clutter.

The bathroom is a fairly recent addition to the house. Until the late nineteenth century, when indoor plumbing became widespread, people used chamber pots or outdoor privies; washing was done indoors using portable tubs or washstands. Thus, the bathrooms in older country houses have usually been converted from what were once small bedrooms or other rooms. As a result, bathrooms may be quite large, and include multiple windows, lots of space, and even a fireplace; or they may be very small. In either case, English country style can be adapted to create a charming bathroom, with floors of wood or tile, and wainscoting or pretty wallpaper on the walls, and incorporating old-fashioned accessories, lots of plush towels, colorful fabrics, and fresh or dried flowers.

ABOVE: *Tongue-and-groove wainscoting surrounds a basic khaki and cream bathroom and encases a bathtub to hide its plumbing fixtures. Decorative elements not typical of bathrooms such as a mix of pictures, a black iron garden chair, and wall-to-wall carpeting show that the room is treated like an extension of the bedroom.*

ABOVE: *Architecture directed the decorating scheme of this handsome bedroom with Tudor-style wood paneled walls and a massive fireplace. The walls' rich brown is set off by white and beige bed linens and off-white carpeting, and is repeated in the furniture choices. The pale color scheme reflects the bright natural light generously provided by a long row of leaded glass windows and keeps the room from becoming dark and heavy.*

ABOVE: *A chic white plaster mirror framed with stylized scrolls is the focal point of this sparsely decorated bathroom. A simple porcelain tub with a hand-held brass showerhead is accompanied by an evocative Victorian wicker chair. The mirror reveals other interesting bathroom fixtures: a Victorian-style toilet tank and vanity.*

RIGHT: *Canvas-colored walls and curtains, and light, pickled floorboards allow disparate objects to work well together, like the red tropical fabric draping a chair, a heavy wood chest with a heraldic motif, and a zigzag rug of bright colors.*

A B O V E : *The well-worn but stately appearance of a master bedroom derives from the generous height of the ceiling and its massive window. Dressed with cotton chintz fabrics, the combination of patterns on the curtains, bed canopy, and upholstered easy chair creates an inviting refuge. The warming effect of the soft red fabrics is enhanced by the yellow-painted walls.*

ABOVE: *A daybed for sitting and sleeping was put in this room which was big enough to hold only a twin bed and little other furniture. Pulled together by a well-chosen mix of blue and cream chintz, the upholstered headboard and custom-made bed canopy and window curtains show that no element of the design was left unconsidered.*

❧

ABOVE: *A sloped roofline is taken advantage of by the attached bed corona, giving the bed a majestic presence.*
A muted-color chintz fabric dominates the decorating scheme and pulls the room together.

OPPOSITE: *Striped wallpaper in two tones of gold enriches a bedroom of harmonious objects, colors, and textures. All-white*
bedding dresses the carved bed to set off its unusually carved headboard and provides a cool balance to the warm tones of the walls
and furniture. An all-brown lamp and shade are well chosen to repeat the rich color of the wooden bed.

ABOVE: *Blue and white porcelains and a sterling silver comb, brush, and mirror are classic embellishments of a skirted bedroom table. Set against a backdrop of floral chintz fabric, the objects represent quintessential English country style.*

OPPOSITE: *A comfortable bedroom's white walls and use of patterned fabric provide a domesticated setting for a restrained display of personal objects. Rows of pictures are neatly arranged according to matting color and size. The table top and mantel are employed as showcases for plates, postcards, small porcelains, and boxes of stationery. Daylight or incandescent lights are used to illuminate the family's collections.*

ABOVE: *A cornflower blue footed bathtub sits on wall-to-wall carpeting that matches the blue and white wide-striped wallpaper in a traditional country bathroom. Personal touches of silver-framed photographs, and cobalt apothecary and perfume containers add to the bathroom's charm.*

ABOVE: *A bathroom shows a Victorian penchant for clutter. A decoupage screen serves only a decorative function in its position between the bathtub and the wall. The clothes rack is hung with arrangements of dried flowers, also serving a decorative function.*

ABOVE: *This all-white rugged cottage bedchamber looks almost Mediterranean with its freshly painted walls and use of blue. Unfinished exposed floors echo the supporting lintels that are embedded in the walls and ceiling.*

RIGHT: *Next to the
gilded side chair and
built-in wardrobe, an
English pine chest of
drawers stores the
overflow of a large
collection of bedding.
The chest blends
visually with the more
ornate pieces because
of its unobtrusive
design and simple
lines.*

OPPOSITE: *A wood bassinet with fresh white linens and a protective mosquito net provides a nestlike cradle for a newborn. Dusty rose walls bring a warm and soothing quality to this nursery.*

RIGHT: *A child's room is casually strewn with antique dolls, miniature furniture, and stuffed animals. When streaming sunlight turns to moonlight, one can imagine that the enchanting nursery takes on a magical quality.*

ABOVE: *Floral chintz fabric covers this matching pair of iron beds and dominates the room's decorating scheme. Window treatments pick up the cool blue of the duvets and coordinate with gray-blue walls. A round-topped center table is dually shared for bedside reading material, a table lamp, and an arrangement of fresh-cut flowers that echoes the chintz.*

OPPOSITE: *A dormer window with a child-size windowseat was fitted with a curtain tailored to the hipped-roof alcove. Cool blue patterned walls bring airiness to the compact space filled with a young girl's toys and a china tea set on loan from Mum.*

OPPOSITE:
*Decorated for
personal pleasure,
a bedroom can be a
gallery that reflects
a collector's love for
artwork. An eclectic
variety of subjects,
styles, sizes, and
mediums is hung
in a balanced
arrangement and
positioned to give
bedside viewers a
good vantage point.
Other cherished pieces
crowd the tabletops
below.*

RIGHT: *In a lady's
boudoir, a white-
painted writing desk
sits in front of a
bedroom window for
natural light. Framed
photographs crowd
every available
surface, adding a
personal touch.*

ABOVE: *Every inch of space is filled on the surface of a woven wicker side table. A traditional collection of blue and white Chinese porcelains, ivory elephants, and bowls of potpourri surrounds a colorful lamp with a fruit-and-leaf motif.*

OPPOSITE: *An iron twin bed sits opposite a small fireplace with a stylized Art Nouveau design. Curves are repeated in the bentwood Thonet-style rocking chair and complement the repetitive hard lines of the bed and the room's irregular walls and ceiling. Yellow wallpaper brings warmth to the oddly shaped space.*

LEFT: *A pale-colored bedroom glows with afternoon sunlight reflected off crisp white bed linens and curtains. The grouping of a variety of furniture styles works because of their carefully planned placement around the central bed and the light sisal carpet, cream walls, and white ceiling.*

ABOVE: *An irregularly shaped bathroom wall is enhanced by the display of different blue and white plates. A series of delft tiles surrounds the wall above the tub and continues behind the sink, creating a backsplash with visual interest. An old standing towel rack stores towels and serves a decorative function.*

ABOVE: *A romantic bedroom's decorating scheme possesses an air of restraint. Putty walls are a sophisticated balance to the feminine lace table covers. The bed covering echoes the look of real lace. The sedate color also sobers the bows that tie back the valances, and keeps the room from seeming overly fussy.*

OPPOSITE: *Exposed pine beams embedded in white stucco are the main attraction in this chalet-style upstairs bedroom. A single framed engraving hung just below the roofline is the only embellishment needed. The casually tossed bright-colored throw blanket stands out confidently among the essential furnishings.*

INDEX

PHOTO CREDITS

Front jacket photograph: Houses & Interiors\Steve Hawkins

Back jacket photograph: Edifice\Phillippa Lewis

Abode: 55, 58, 63, 70, 80, 85

Arcaid: ©Julie Phipps: 33 right (Designer: Shirley Ann Sell)

©Edifice\Darley: 26–27

©Edifice\Jackson: 16–17

©Edifice\Lewis: 2, 8, 19 right, 20 both, 24, 26 left

Elizabeth Whiting & Associates: 30; ©Peter Aprahamian: 67; ©Nick Carter: 42 bottom (Designer: Amanda Baird); ©Michael Dunne: 84; ©Brian Harrison: 12 (Designer: Giles Wyatt Smith), ©Dennis Stone: 94; ©Simon Upton: 44–45 (Designer: Thelma and Johnny Morris), 56–57 (Designer: Robin Parish), 64; ©Andreas von Einsiedel: 54, 71

Houses & Interiors: 68, 75, 91, ©Steve Hawkins: 40

©Ken Kirkwood: 5, 14, 18, 21, 22, 23 top, 32, 57 right, 60, 61, 62, 81, 82, 93 right

©image/dennis krukowski: 19 left (Designer: Tonin MAC Callum, ASID, Inc.), 86 (Designer: Mary Meehan, Interiors, Inc.)

The Interior Archive: ©Tim Beddow: 10–11, 83, 87, 92–93; ©Simon Brown: 37 bottom, 74; ©James Mortimer: 39 (Designer: Stanley Falconer), 41 bottom (Designer: Steve Falconer), 76 (Designer Stanley Falconer); ©J. Pilkington: 33 left (Designer: Jeremy Fry), 50 top (Designer: Lucy Ward), 66 bottom (Designer: Lorranine Kirk), 72 left (Designer: Lorraine Kirk), 72–73 (Designer: Lorraine Kirk), 89 (Designer: Lorraine Kirk); ©C. Simon Sykes: 7, 34–35, 37 top, 38, 48, 65, 66 top, 88, 90, ©Fritz von de Schulenburg: 13, 23 bottom, 25, 28 (Designer: Sam Chesterton), 31, 35 right (Designer: Emily Todhunter), 36, 41 top, 42 top, 43, 45 right, 46 both, 47, 49 (Designer: Emily Todhunter), 50 bottom, 51, 52, 59, 77, 78, 79 (Vicki Rothco), 95 (Designer: Emily Todhunter)